Book A

LANGUAGE
Power

gagelearning

Copyright © 2002 Gage Learning Corporation

1120 Birchmount Road, Toronto, Ontario M1K 5G4   1-800-668-0671

www.nelson.com

Adapted from material developed, designed, and copyrighted by Steck-Vaughn.

Editorial Team: Chelsea Donaldson, Carol Waldock
Cover Adaptation: Christine Dandurand

ISBN-13: **978-0-7715-1013-7**
ISBN-10: **0-7715-1013-6**

6 7 8 9 WC 09 08 07 06
Printed and bound in Canada

Table of Contents

Unit 5   Composition

Unit 6   Study Skills

Final Reviews

> ■ A **synonym** is a word that means almost the same thing as another word.
>
> EXAMPLE: small—little, jump—leap

■ **Write a synonym for each word shown under the lines. Choose synonyms from the box.**

Many people have heard _____
　　　　　　　　　　　　　　(tales)

about the Cyclops. He was a _____
　　　　　　　　　　　　　　　　(large)

monster. He had a body like a _____ .
　　　　　　　　　　　　　　　　　(human)

But his face was _____ . He had only
　　　　　　　　　　　(different)

one eye in the _____ of his forehead.
　　　　　　　　　(centre)

His _____ was a cave on an
　　　(house)

island. The people who lived near the island were

_____ of the Cyclops. He was
　　(scared)

very mean and _____ .
　　　　　　　　　(loud)

afraid
huge
person
home
stories
unusual
middle
noisy

■ **Write a sentence using the synonyms <u>funny</u> and <u>silly</u>. Tell about something you like.**

_____

_____

Unit 1, Vocabulary　　　　　　　**1**

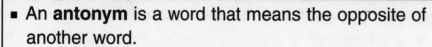

> ■ An **antonym** is a word that means the opposite of another word.
>
> EXAMPLES: on—off, wet—dry

■ **Write an antonym for each word shown under the lines. Choose the antonyms from the box.**

play small easy long fun back

A gerbil is a _____ , furry
                    (large)

animal. It has long _____ legs. Its
                          (front)

tail is _____ and hairy. A gerbil is
            (short)

_____ to care for, and it is a
         (hard)

_____ pet. It loves to
         (boring)

_____ .
         (work)

■ **Write the sentences. Complete each one with an antonym for the underlined word.**

1. Do you think Ann will <u>win</u> or (lose, leave)?

   _____

   _____

2. Will he do a backbend <u>now</u> or (never, later)?

   _____

   _____

> • A **homonym** is a word that sounds the same as another word but has a different spelling and a different meaning.
>
> EXAMPLES: **they're**, **their**, **there**
> Use they're to mean "they are."
> **They're** playing now.
> Use their to mean "belonging to them."
> Did they bring **their** bats?
> Use there to mean "in that place" or to help begin a thought.
> He threw it **there**. **There** are two teams.

• **Write they're, their, or there.**

1. Lee and Vin raced down the street carrying

   _____ baseball gloves.

2. "All the players are _____ ,
   in the park," yelled Lee.

3. "I hope _____ ready for the
   big game today," said Vin.

4. All the players quickly took _____ places on
   the field.

5. "Look, _____ are people cheering for us!" cried Vin.

6. "I think _____ here to see us win the game," said Lee.

7. Vin and Lee's team won _____ game by one point.

• **Write a sentence about a baseball game using they're,
their, or there.**

_____

More Homonyms

- Remember that a homonym is a word that sounds the same as another word.

  EXAMPLES: **hear**, **here**   **to**, **two**, **too**

  Use <u>hear</u> to mean "to listen to."
  Did you **hear** that funny song?
  Use <u>here</u> to mean "in this place."
  The tapes are over **here**.
  Use <u>to</u> to mean "toward" or to go with words like <u>make</u> and <u>buy</u>.
  Juan rode his bike **to** the store. He wanted **to** buy a tape.
  Use <u>too</u> to mean "more than enough" or "also."
  The music is **too** loud. I like that song, **too**.
  Use <u>two</u> to mean "the number 2."
  Those **two** speakers sound very good.

- **Underline the correct homonym.**

  1. Put the new speakers over (hear, here).

  2. Listen (to, too, two) the soft music.

  3. Do you (hear, here) the band playing?

  4. Those (to, too, two) compact discs were on sale.

  5. Dad bought some tapes, (to, too, two).

  6. We will dance when we (hear, here) the music.

  7. Mom will come in (to, too, two) watch us.

  8. (Here, Hear) comes Dad to show us a dance.

  9. His (to, too, two) feet just float across the floor.

  10. Do you (hear, here) us clapping for him?

- **Use <u>hear</u> and <u>here</u> in a sentence about music.**

Words with More Than One Meaning

> ■ Many words have more than one meaning.
> EXAMPLE: <u>Pound</u> means "hit hard over and over."
> **Pound** the stake into the ground. <u>Pound</u> also
> means "an enclosed place in which to keep stray
> animals." The dog was taken to the **pound**.

■ **Read the meanings on the right. Write the number
of the meaning for each underlined word.**

1. My little brother was playing with his

   spinning <u>top</u>. _____

2. Mom asked him to turn on the outside <u>light</u>. _____

3. The strong wind had turned over the <u>light</u>

   doghouse. _____

4. I heard the dog <u>bark</u> at the squirrel. _____

5. It was climbing up the <u>bark</u> of the tree. _____

6. The squirrel went to the <u>top</u> of the tree. _____

7. It was <u>light</u> enough to jump onto a thin

   branch. _____

8. But there wasn't enough <u>light</u> to see where the

   squirrel went next. _____

<u>light</u>
1. not heavy
2. something that
   helps us to see
<u>bark</u>
1. hard outside
   covering of a
   tree
2. the sound a
   dog makes
<u>top</u>
1. the highest part
2. a toy

■ **Write a sentence using the first meaning of <u>light</u>.**

_____

_____

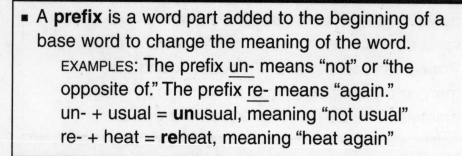

- A **prefix** is a word part added to the beginning of a base word to change the meaning of the word.
  EXAMPLES: The prefix un- means "not" or "the opposite of." The prefix re- means "again."
  un- + usual = **un**usual, meaning "not usual"
  re- + heat = **re**heat, meaning "heat again"

- **Add the prefix un- to the words below.
  Then write the meaning of the new word.**

1. happy _____ _____
2. fair _____ _____
3. even _____ _____
4. safe _____ _____
5. tie _____ _____

- **Add the prefix re- to the words below.
  Then write the meaning of the new word.**

1. open _____ _____
2. test _____ _____
3. use _____ _____
4. read _____ _____

- **Write one sentence with a word that has the prefix un-.
  Write one sentence with a word that has the prefix re-.**

1. _____
2. _____

> ▪ A **suffix** is a word part added to the end of a base word to change the meaning of the word.
>
> EXAMPLES: The suffixes <u>-er</u> and <u>-or</u> mean "a person or thing that _____ ."
>
> heat + -er = heat**er**, meaning "a thing that heats"
>
> sail + -or = sail**or**, meaning "a person that sails"

▪ **Add the suffixes to the words to make new words.**

1. climb + er = _____   **5.** act + or = _____

2. teach + er = _____   **6.** mark + er = _____

3. visit + or = _____   **7.** paint + er = _____

4. print + er = _____   **8.** sing + er = _____

▪ **Write each sentence with a new word made by adding <u>-er</u> to the word in ( ).**

1. The _____ clipped the roses.   (garden)

_____

2. He cleaned his gloves in the clothes _____ .   (wash)

_____

3. He and a _____ ate lunch.   (farm)

_____

4. Then he bought a new _____ for his seeds.   (plant)

_____

5. The gardener used to be a _____ .   (teach)

_____

> ■ A **compound word** is made by joining one word with another word.
>   EXAMPLE: air + plane = airplane

■ **Write the compound word made by joining each pair of words.**

1. birth + day =

_____

2. after + noon =

_____

3. skate + board =

_____

4. fire + place =

_____

5. cat + fish =

_____

6. rain + bow =

_____

7. snow + ball =

_____

8. sun + rise =

_____

9. water + fall =

_____

10. down + stairs =

_____

■ **Underline the compound word in each sentence.
Then write the two words that form the compound word.**

1. The birthday party is a surprise.   _____ _____

2. Is everyone here?   _____ _____

3. Let's run downstairs and hide!   _____ _____

4. Everything is ready.   _____ _____

5. The party is for a classmate.   _____ _____

6. I brought a football as a gift.   _____ _____

Unit 1, Vocabulary

> ■ A **contraction** is a word made by joining two words. When the words are joined, a letter or letters are left out. An **apostrophe** (') shows where the missing letter or letters would be.
>
> EXAMPLES: I + will = I'll, there + is = there's, is + not = isn't

■ **Rewrite the sentences. Use contractions in place of the underlined words.**

doesn't	Here's	I'll	isn't	she'll	She's	There's

1. She is going camping this weekend.

   _____

2. I think she will go fishing in the lake.

   _____

3. Inuk does not like to fish.

   _____

4. Here is some fresh bait.

   _____

5. There is enough for everyone to use.

   _____

6. After we catch the fish, I will help cook them.

   _____

7. It is not hard to do.

   _____

■ **Write a sentence telling what you will do this weekend. Use the contraction I'll.**

_____

■ **Write the synonym for each underlined word.**

1. We went into the <u>big</u> circus tent. (tiny, huge) _____

2. The acrobats' tricks looked <u>hard</u>. (difficult, easy) _____

3. They can <u>jump</u> high into the air. (crawl, leap) _____

4. Our seats were at the <u>back</u>. (rear, front) _____

5. We <u>liked</u> all the acts. (hated, enjoyed) _____

■ **Write the antonym for each underlined word.**

1. Is the clown act <u>first</u> or (never, last)? _____

2. The clown is <u>happy</u>, but has a (sad, red) face. _____

3. Her nose is <u>big</u>, but her ears are (small, flat). _____

4. She has a <u>narrow</u> tie and (skinny, wide) shoes. _____

5. Was the clown's wink <u>fast</u> or (quick, slow)? _____

■ **Choose and underline the correct word in each sentence.**

1. The juggler is over (here, hear).

2. He likes talking (too, to, two) the crowd.

3. There are only (to, two, too) acts left.

4. (They're, Their, There) about to begin.

5. The stars take (they're, their, there) final bows.

6. Darla has fun at the circus, (to, too, two).

7. There are many things to see and (here, hear).

- **Write two sentences. Use a different meaning for <u>beat</u> in each sentence.**

  1. _____

  2. _____

- **Write two sentences. Use a different meaning for <u>match</u> in each sentence.**

  1. _____

  2. _____

- **Underline each word that begins with a prefix.**

  1. pack, unpack   4. relive, live   7. rename, name

  2. copy, recopy   5. make, remake   8. true, untrue

  3. untie, tie   6. take, retake   9. unsure, sure

- **Underline each word that ends with a suffix.**

  1. clean, cleaner   4. teacher, teach   7. heater, heat

  2. visitor, visit   5. dry, dryer   8. lead, leader

  3. work, worker   6. act, actor   9. sailor, sail

- **Underline each contraction. Circle each compound word.**

  1. There's the tightrope.   4. We can't see everything.

  2. We'll be inside the tent.   5. Let's eat something.

  3. The clown isn't in the airplane.   6. Doesn't everyone like the circus?

■ **Rewrite the letter. Use a homonym for the words in dark print. Use a contraction for the words that are underlined.**

> Dear Tom,
>   It was very hot **hear** in the house today. I went **too** the pool **too** cool off. My **to** friends, Anna and Rosa, were **their**. We <u>did</u> <u>not</u> do anything but swim. <u>We</u> <u>will</u> go back tomorrow. I **here** <u>it</u> <u>will</u> be even hotter then. <u>I</u> <u>will</u> be sure to tell Anna and Rosa to bring **they're** beach ball.

_____

_____

_____

_____

_____

_____

_____

_____

- **Write a story about summer fun. Include these words in your story:**

  1. a synonym of <u>bright</u>
  2. an antonym of <u>cold</u>
  3. the homonyms <u>pale</u>, <u>pail</u>
  4. a compound word
  5. a word with the prefix <u>re-</u> or <u>un-</u>
  6. a word with the suffix <u>-er</u> or <u>-or</u>

_____

_____

_____

_____

_____

_____

_____

_____

_____

_____

_____

_____

_____

_____

_____

_____

_____

_____

- A **sentence** is a group of words that tells or asks something. It stands for a complete thought.
  EXAMPLE: Sally dreamed about the picnic.

- **Underline the sentences.**

1. Eva and Sue ate fried chicken.
2. Smelled good to eat.
3. Did Sue find the rolls?
4. Sue and Eva?

5. Eva ran to get swing.
6. Swung up to the stars.
7. Is Sue hungry again?
8. Potato salad.

- **Match each group of words in A with a group of words in B to make a complete sentence. Write the sentences below.**

A	B
The ants	looking for crumbs.
They were	marched in a row.
Eva	saw them coming.
She moved	was for Eva, not the ants.
The food	her blanket right away.

1. _____

2. _____

3. _____

4. _____

5. _____

> ■ Remember that a sentence is a group of words that tells or asks something. It stands for a complete thought.

■ **Choose the sentence in each pair of word groups below. Write the sentence.**

1. Catherine saw Superdog. A most unusual dog.

   _____

2. Flew high as a rocket. Superdog flew high.

   _____

3. Where is Superdog? Superdog with his trainer?

   _____

4. Superdog read about the dog show. The big show.

   _____

5. Went to the show. Superdog went to the show.

   _____

6. Win a ribbon? Did he win a blue ribbon?

   _____

7. Superdog won "Best of Show." "Best of Show."

   _____

■ **Read the paragraph below. Draw a line through each group of words that is not a sentence.**

Catherine and Superdog walked to the dog show.

What did Superdog do there? Surprised all the judges.

The judges in the chairs. Superdog ran as fast as a

train. Jumped over a tall building in a single bound.

Statements and Questions

> - Some sentences are **statements**. They tell something.
>   EXAMPLE: This is a totem pole.
> - Some sentences are **questions**. They ask something.
>   EXAMPLE: Is this a totem pole?

- **Write <u>S</u> in front of each statement.**
  Write <u>Q</u> in front of each question.

_____ 1. I am reading about totem poles.

_____ 2. Have you ever seen one?

_____ 3. Northwest Coast First Nations people carved totem poles.

_____ 4. Animals often appear on the poles.

_____ 5. Did you know they often tell a story?

_____ 6. Some are more than fifteen metres high.

_____ 7. In the past, many poles were destroyed.

_____ 8. Now new ones are being carved.

_____ 9. Aren't these ones beautiful?

_____ 10. Would you like to borrow the book?

- **Copy the sentences below. Underline the
  statement once. Underline the question twice.**

  Many people visit museums to see totem poles. Have you
  ever been to a museum?

_____

_____

_____

Unit 2, Sentences

- Some sentences are **commands**. They tell somebody to do something.

    EXAMPLE: Squeeze all the juice out of the lemons.

- Some sentences are **exclamations**. They show strong feelings or surprise.

    EXAMPLE: What a sour taste that lemon has!

- **Write C in front of each command. Write E in front of each exclamation.**

_____ 1. How delicious those strawberries look!

_____ 2. Slice the bananas.

_____ 3. Add the water to the mix.

_____ 4. What a great lunch we'll have outside!

_____ 5. Clean the grill well.

_____ 6. How golden that chicken is!

_____ 7. Pass the salad, please.

_____ 8. The ants got the cake!

_____ 9. What a good idea this picnic was!

- **Write a sentence that is a command. Tell somebody to do the first step in making your favourite food.**

_____

- **Write a sentence that is an exclamation. Write what you would say after eating something good.**

_____

Lesson 14 Subjects in Sentences

> ■ A sentence has two parts. One part is called the **subject**. The subject tells who or what the sentence is about. EXAMPLE: **The snow** is deep.

■ **Underline the subject in each sentence.**

1. We went tobogganing today.
2. The toboggan flew down the hill.
3. Jamie threw a snowball.
4. Kamal lost his hat.
5. Skaters were on the pond.
6. The ice was smooth.
7. Alan liked to spin around.
8. He went very fast.
9. Our friends slid by us.
10. A red glove was in the snow.

■ **Complete each sentence by adding a subject.**

1. _____ put on her ice skates.
2. _____ helped his little sister.
3. _____ sat on the sled.
4. _____ went down the hill.
5. _____ was very cold.
6. _____ watched the snow fall.
7. _____ liked the snow.
8. _____ makes tracks in the snow.
9. _____ are on the ice.
10. _____ can skate well.
11. _____ turned to the left.
12. _____ went home.

> ■ A sentence has two parts. One part is called the subject. The other part is called the **predicate**. The predicate tells what the subject is, was, or does.
> EXAMPLE: That big zoo **is nearby**.

■ **Underline the predicate in each sentence.**

1. The cub growled at the bird.
2. The huge ape swung from a bar.
3. Barry liked the camels.
4. These tiny snakes are harmless.
5. Monkeys are fun to watch.

6. Vic petted the sheep.
7. A calf was in the yard.
8. Mario saw the baby ducks.
9. The pigs cooled off.
10. An owl hooted softly.

■ **Complete each sentence by adding a predicate.**

1. The clucking chickens _____.

2. The baby goats _____.

3. Barbara _____.

4. All the elephants _____.

5. A zookeeper _____.

6. The bears _____.

7. Those tigers _____.

8. Many people _____.

9. A sleeping bat _____.

10. The balloon man _____.

11. Everyone _____.

> - Two short sentences with the same predicate can be **combined** to make a new sentence. The two parts are joined by and.   EXAMPLE: Lou laughed. + Gina laughed. → Lou **and** Gina laughed.
> - Two short sentences with the same subject can be combined to make a new sentence. The two parts are joined by and.   EXAMPLE: Fred counted his coins. + Fred paid for the tickets. → Fred counted his coins **and** paid for the tickets.

- **Combine the sentences. Write the new sentence.**

1. Mom went on the ride. Trish went on the ride.

   _____

2. Bob stood in line. The boys stood in line.

   _____

3. Luke ate lunch. Jung ate lunch.

   _____

4. Donna took a picture. Donna sat down to rest.

   _____

5. Ed popped the balloons. Ed won a prize.

   _____

6. Linda went to the petting zoo. Linda fed the animals.

   _____

   _____

7. Ryan saw the bears. Ryan rode on the train.

   _____

> - Two short sentences that closely share an idea can be combined to make one sentence.
> - The two sentences may be joined with connecting words such as <u>or</u>, <u>and</u>, or <u>but</u>. A comma is placed before these words.
>
>   EXAMPLES: Tony found shells. + Amy caught seaweed. →
>   Tony found shells, **and** Amy caught seaweed.
>   I can't swim. + I can wade. →
>   I can't swim, **but** I can wade.
>   Fish from here. + Go to the dock. →
>   Fish from here, **or** go to the dock.

- **Underline the two short sentences that were combined to make each sentence.**

  1. The wind howled, and the sand blew around.

  2. The children can swim, or they can play ball.

  3. The water is cold but the sand is warm.

  4. The sea is blue, and the foam is white.

  5. Dad carried our lunch, and we carried the chairs.

- **Combine the sentences using the word in ( ). Write the new sentence.**

  1. Take your pail. Fill it with sand.   (and)

  _____

  2. You can make a castle. You can make a cave.   (or)

  _____

  3. We can't play on rocks. We can play on sand.   (but)

  _____

■ If a sentence tells about more than one main idea, it
should be rewritten as two sentences.
EXAMPLE: Most plants have seeds, some seeds
are good to eat. → Most plants have seeds.
Some seeds are good to eat.

■ **Read the sentences. Write two sentences for each.**

1. The seeds must be planted, this is done
   in many ways.

   _____

   _____

2. A seed floated in the breeze, it was
   very windy.

   _____

   _____

3. You can eat these seeds, Shameka will
   gather some more.

   _____

   _____

4. Birds and animals eat seeds, you can buy
   seeds for them in a store.

   _____

   _____

- **For each pair, underline the group of words that is a sentence.**

    1. Owls have large eyes. Catch food at night.

    2. Huge whales. They live in the ocean.

    3. Lizards are reptiles. Are cold-blooded.

    4. What do chipmunks? Do you like chipmunks?

- **Write S in front of each statement. Write Q in front of each question.**

    _____ 1. Why did the kitten buy a fan?

    _____ 2. It wanted to be a cool cat.

    _____ 3. How did the heater make the dog feel?

    _____ 4. The heater made it feel like a hot dog.

- **Write C in front of each command. Write E in front of each exclamation.**

    _____ 1. Give the cat its food.

    _____ 2. What beautiful fur your cat has!

    _____ 3. Don't let the cat go outside.

    _____ 4. Your cat is so playful!

- **Underline the subject. Circle the predicate.**

    1. The cat washed its face with its paw.

    2. Kirk threw a ball of yarn to the cat.

    3. The cat took a long nap.

    4. Kirk fed the cat after its nap.

- **Combine the sentences to make a new sentence.**

1. Erin fed her mouse. Erin cleaned its cage.

   _____

   _____

2. Raul held the mouse. Ann held the mouse.

   _____

   _____

3. The mouse feels warm. Its nose feels cool.

   _____

   _____

   _____

- **Read the sentences. Write two sentences for each.**

1. My friend comes over, my dad takes us to see a movie.

   _____

   _____

2. We stand in line, we get our tickets.

   _____

   _____

3. We find a place to sit, we share some popcorn.

   _____

   _____

4. The theatre gets dark, the movie begins.

   _____

   _____

- **Rewrite the story below, but make it less choppy. Combine each pair of sentences that is underlined. When you are finished, you will have six sentences in all.**

> The sea horse is an amazing animal! It is only about ten centimetres tall. It is covered with bony plates. The sea horse swims by using the fin on its back. It is not a strong swimmer. Ocean currents carry it. They move the sea horse from one place to another. The sea horse can easily stop itself. It just wraps its tail around a sea plant.

_____

_____

_____

_____

_____

_____

_____

_____

_____

_____

- **Write a story about another animal that lives in the sea. Use at least two statements, one question, and one exclamation.**

_____

_____

_____

_____

_____

_____

_____

- **Imagine you are a diver. Write a story about the things you saw when you were diving in the ocean. Use at least two statements, one question, and one exclamation.**

_____

_____

_____

_____

_____

_____

_____

- A **noun** is a word that names a person, place, or thing. The words <u>a</u>, <u>an</u>, and <u>the</u> are clues that show a noun is near.

    EXAMPLES: a pilot, the moon, the island

- **Underline the two nouns in each sentence.**

    1. The astronaut looked out the window.

    2. Clouds circled the earth.

    3. The ocean looked like a lake.

    4. Another astronaut ate her lunch.

    5. An apple floated inside the cabin.

    6. One man put on his spacesuit.

    7. The astronaut walked in space.

    8. The newspaper had pictures of him.

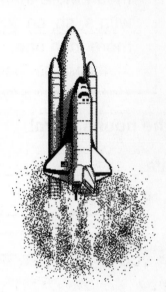

- **Write a noun from the list to complete each sentence.**

best	ocean	radio
cheer	happy	ship
day	hear	tall
doctor	over	the

1. They landed in the _____ .

2. A _____ sailed over to them.

3. The _____ checked their health.

4. The news was on the _____ .

5. We all let out a _____ .

6. It was an exciting _____ .

Lesson 20

Singular and Plural Nouns

- A **singular noun** names one person, place, or thing.
  EXAMPLES: bee, fox, bench
- A **plural noun** names more than one person, place, or thing. Add -s to most nouns to change them to mean more than one. Add -es to nouns that end with s, sh, ch, x, or z to change them to mean more than one.
  EXAMPLES: bees, foxes, benches

- **Make the nouns plural.**

1. skate _____

2. car _____

3. parade _____

4. toe _____

5. brush _____

6. class _____

7. witch _____

8. box _____

9. dish _____

10. dollar _____

11. leash _____

12. watch _____

- **Rewrite each sentence. Choose the correct noun in ( ).**

1. The fish are in a new (tank, tanks).

   _____

2. All the (plant, plants) are fresh.

   _____

3. Use that (net, nets) to catch the fish.

   _____

4. Both those (boy, boys) visit the fish store.

   _____

© 1997 Gage Educational Publishing Company   Unit 3, Grammar and Usage

Common and Proper Nouns

- A **proper noun** names a particular person, place, or thing. It begins with a capital letter.
  EXAMPLES: Wayne Gretzky, Edmonton, Park School
- A **common noun** does not name a particular person, place, or thing.
  EXAMPLES: athlete, city, school

- **Write C for a common noun. Write P for a proper noun.**

_____ **1.** girl

_____ **2.** Mexico

_____ **3.** mountain

_____ **4.** country

_____ **5.** Alberta

_____ **6.** Eaton's

_____ **7.** lake

_____ **8.** Terry Fox

_____ **9.** Friday

_____ **10.** Rocky Mountains

_____ **11.** building

_____ **12.** doctor

- **Read the sentences. Draw one line under the common noun. Circle the proper noun.**

1. The ocean was very rough on Tuesday.

2. The waves pounded Cavendish Beach.

3. The beach is on Prince Edward Island.

4. Some children were there from Halifax.

5. Pierre spied a seaplane.

6. Its name was Flying Gull.

7. The plane was flying to New Brunswick.

8. Franca waved to the pilot.

Lesson 22

Action Verbs

> - A **verb** usually shows action. It tells what a person, place, or thing is or was doing.
>   EXAMPLES: The cub **sleeps** in the shade.
>   A tiger **ran** across the field.

- **Underline the verb in each sentence.**

1. A beautiful bird chattered in the forest.

2. Elephants drank from the stream.

3. An animal leaped in the air.

4. Meg read this in a book about Africa.

5. She got it from the library.

- **Choose a verb from the list to complete each sentence.**

buzz grow roar search swing

1. We _____ for butterflies.

2. Many plants _____ by the stream.

3. Monkeys _____ from branches.

4. The insects _____ around us.

5. The lions _____ loudly.

- **Use an action verb in a sentence about animals in Africa.**

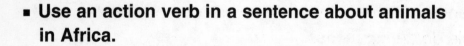

_____

_____

- Verbs can show that an action happens in the **present**.
  EXAMPLE: The game **starts** now.
- Verbs in the present used with singular subjects,
  except I and you, end in -s.
  EXAMPLES: Troy **likes** to pitch. I **like** to pitch.
- Verbs in the present used with plural subjects have no
  special endings.   EXAMPLE: The girls **play** kickball.

- **Complete each sentence with the correct verb.**

1. The bell _____ at 10:00. (ring, rings)

2. The children _____ outside to play. (run, runs)

3. Gabriela _____ to Jenny. (wave, waves)

4. The students _____ to their friends. (talk, talks)

5. The new girl _____ at the ball. (swing, swings)

6. My teacher _____ us laugh. (make, makes)

7. Claude _____ a joke. (tell, tells)

8. The players _____ for the game. (plan, plans)

- **Write sentences with verbs in the present.**

1. Tell what you do during recess at school.

   _____

   _____

2. Tell what other people do during recess.

   _____

   _____

Verbs in the Past

> ■ Verbs can show that an action happened in the **past**. Add the endings -d or -ed to most verbs to show that something happened in the past.
>
> EXAMPLE: Yesterday we **washed** our bikes.

■ **Underline the verb in each sentence. Write P in front of each sentence with a verb in the past.**

_____ 1. My friends like to ride to the park.

_____ 2. The wheels turned around and around.

_____ 3. They stopped at the light.

_____ 4. I squeezed the black handlebars.

_____ 5. We pedal as far as we can.

_____ 6. They rested for half an hour.

■ **Rewrite the sentences. Change each verb from the present to the past by adding -d or -ed.**

1. We enter the bike race.

_____

2. We start the race together.

_____

3. We walk our bikes up the hill.

_____

4. The dogs chase our wheels.

_____

5. I hope to win.

_____

Lesson 25

Linking Verbs

> ■ A **linking verb** does not show action. It links, or joins, the subject to a word in the predicate. Verbs such as <u>am</u>, <u>is</u>, <u>are</u>, <u>was</u>, and <u>were</u> are linking verbs.
> EXAMPLES: Those insects **are** crickets.
> They **were** noisy.

■ **Write <u>L</u> in front of each sentence that has a linking verb.**

_____ 1. The crickets are loud tonight.

_____ 2. They chirp in the grass.

_____ 3. The dogs bark at the cars.

_____ 4. They were quiet earlier.

_____ 5. An owl screeches in the tree.

_____ 6. It is afraid of the dogs.

_____ 7. The white cat meows at her kitten.

_____ 8. She tells it not to wander.

_____ 9. The birds are asleep in their nests.

_____ 10. A jet roars over the house.

_____ 11. Everyone is quiet inside.

_____ 12. Just listen to the sounds at night!

■ **Use a linking verb in a sentence that tells about another sound you can hear at night.**

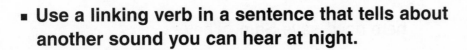

_____

> - Use <u>am</u> with the word I.
>   EXAMPLE: I **am** ready to go fishing.
> - Use <u>is</u> with one person, place, or thing.
>   EXAMPLE: Joe **is** ready to go, too.
> - Use <u>are</u> with more than one and with the word <u>you</u>.
>   EXAMPLES: We **are** all ready now.
>   **Are** you ready to go?

- **Write <u>am</u>, <u>is</u>, or <u>are</u>.**

The children _____ fishing. Joe _____ the first

to catch a fish.

He says, "It _____ too small. I will put it back into

the water. When I _____ a few years older, I might

catch it again!"

"You _____ smart," says Mary. "It _____ good

to throw fish back when they are too small."

"I _____ sure I have something big!" shouts Sam.

Mary and Joe help Sam pull the fish into the boat.

"That _____ not a fish," says Mary. She holds up

an old tin can. "People spoil our fishing spot with junk. I

_____ ready to put up a 'No Dumping' sign here."

"Two signs _____ here now," says Sam. "They

_____ over there behind that pile of junk!"

Unit 3, Grammar and Usage

- Use <u>was</u> and <u>were</u> to tell about the past.
- Use <u>was</u> with one person, place, or thing.
  EXAMPLE: Chris **was** busy in the kitchen.
- Use <u>were</u> with more than one and with the word <u>you</u>.
  EXAMPLES: The dishes **were** in the sink.
  We **were** glad that you **were** here to help.

- **Write <u>was</u> or <u>were</u>.**

1. Ben _____ making a house for his dog.

2. He _____ working on it in the garage.

3. The boards _____ too long.

4. The saw _____ sharp.

5. Ben _____ using a saw to cut the boards.

6. Then he _____ looking for the nails.

7. Where _____ the nails?

8. They _____ behind the boards.

9. Ben _____ careful when he used the hammer.

10. Then all the boards _____ nailed in place.

11. Ben _____ ready to paint the doghouse.

12. Blue _____ his favourite colour.

13. Ben hoped that blue _____ his
    dog's favourite colour, too.

14. Ben and his dog _____ excited about
    the new doghouse.

Helping Verbs

> ▪ A **helping verb** helps the main verb. Have, has, or had helps a main verb show action in the past.
>
> EXAMPLES: Rita has moved to a cottage.
> They have packed their bags.
> The farmer had milked the

▪ **Underline the helping verb. Circle the main verb.**

1. The sun has risen.

2. The rooster had remembered to crow.

3. The cows have chewed their grass.

4. The children had collected the eggs.

5. Dad has baked some fresh bread.

6. We have eaten breakfast.

▪ **Rewrite the sentences using the correct verb in ( ).**

1. I (has, have) bought an umbrella.

   _____

2. Pat (has, have) decided to buy one too.

   _____

3. It (has, had) rained a lot lately.

   _____

4. The rain (has, had) soaked us both.

   _____

Lesson 29

Using Forms of *Do* and *See*

- Use <u>does</u> with a singular noun to show the present.
  - EXAMPLE: Anna **does** all the costumes.
- Use <u>do</u> with <u>I</u>, <u>you</u>, and plural subjects to show the present.
  - EXAMPLE: Alan and Lyn **do** want to see the play.
- Use <u>did</u> without a helping verb to show the past.
  - EXAMPLE: Ed **did** a play about pets.
- Use <u>done</u> with a helping verb to show the past.
  - EXAMPLE: Jenna has **done** her part.

■ **Underline the correct verb.**

1. Our group (done, did) a project.

2. We had (done, did) one section.

3. Jo (does, do) well at writing.

4. Bob had (did, done) the pictures.

5. We all (does, do) our part.

6. I (do, does) like to read.

- Use <u>sees</u> with a singular noun to show the present.
  - EXAMPLE: Anna **sees** a runner.
- Use <u>see</u> with <u>I</u>, <u>you</u>, and plural subjects to show the present.
  - EXAMPLE: Alan and Lyn **see** the first runners.
- Use <u>saw</u> without a helping verb to show the past.
  - EXAMPLE: Ed **saw** the high jump contest.
- Use <u>seen</u> with a helping verb to show the past.
  - EXAMPLE: Jenna has **seen** a lot of track meets.

■ **Underline the correct verb.**

1. We (saw, seen) a track meet today.

2. Mom said, "I (see, sees) our seats."

3. We (saw, seen) the high jump contest.

4. Di (sees, see) the last winner.

5. We all shouted, "I (see, sees) the prizes!"

6. The runners had (seen, saw) the crowd.

- Use <u>gives</u> with a singular noun to show the present.
  EXAMPLE: Anna **gives** the actors a gift.
- Use <u>give</u> with <u>I</u>, <u>you</u>, and plural subjects to show the present.
  EXAMPLE: Alan and Lyn **give** helpful tips to the actors.
- Use <u>gave</u> without a helping verb to show the past.
  EXAMPLE: Ed **gave** a speech before the play.
- Use <u>given</u> with a helping verb to show the past.
  EXAMPLE: Jenna had **given** a speech last year.

- **Underline the correct verb.**

1. They (give, gives) the book.

2. Kim (give, gives) a lot of help.

3. Our coach (gave, given) a speech.

4. He has (gave, given) it already.

5. Jim had (gave, given) a speech.

6. Our teacher (gives, give) prizes.

7. We have (gave, given) her flowers.

8. The crowd (gave, given) a cheer.

- Use <u>goes</u> with a singular noun to show the present.
  EXAMPLE: Anna **goes** to the zoo.
- Use <u>go</u> with <u>I</u>, <u>you</u>, and plural subjects to show the present.
  EXAMPLE: Alan and Lyn **go** to the zoo often.
- Use <u>went</u> without a helping verb to show the past.
  EXAMPLE: Ed **went** to the children's zoo.
- Use <u>gone</u> with a helping verb to show the past.
  EXAMPLE: Jenna has **gone** with Ed.

- **Underline the correct verb.**

1. We (go, goes) to the zoo.

2. Ying (go, goes) with her family.

3. I have (gone, went) there before.

4. Our class (go, goes) this week.

5. Ann and Jill (go, goes) together.

6. Tim (went, gone) last year.

7. We (go, goes) in the spring.

8. You (gone, went) with us.

- A **pronoun** is a word that takes the place of a noun.
- Pronouns that take the place of singular nouns are
  <u>I</u>, <u>me</u>, <u>you</u>, <u>he</u>, <u>him</u>, <u>she</u>, <u>her</u>, and <u>it</u>.
  EXAMPLE: **Dave** ate slowly. **He** ate slowly.
- Pronouns that take the place of plural nouns are
  <u>we</u>, <u>us</u>, <u>you</u>, <u>they</u>, and <u>them</u>.
  EXAMPLE: The popcorn is for **the boys**.
  The popcorn is for **them**.

- **Choose the correct pronoun in ( ) to take the place
  of the underlined noun. Then rewrite the sentences.**

  1. <u>Mrs. Cantu</u> made popcorn for the class. (She, They)

  _____

  2. <u>Children</u> love to eat popcorn. (She, They)

  _____

  3. Hot air tosses <u>popcorn</u> around. (it, them)

  _____

  4. <u>Roger</u> put salt on his popcorn. (He, They)

  _____

  5. Don gave some popcorn to <u>Colleen</u>. (her, them)

  _____

  6. Pina gave bowls to <u>Bill</u> and <u>Armand</u>. (it, them)

  _____

- **Write two sentences using pronouns.**

  1. _____

  2. _____

- Use these pronouns as **subjects**: I, <u>you</u>, <u>he</u>, <u>she</u>, <u>it</u>, <u>we</u>, and <u>they</u>.   EXAMPLE: I like stories.
- Use these pronouns as **objects** that follow an action verb: <u>me</u>, <u>you</u>, <u>him</u>, <u>her</u>, <u>it</u>, <u>us</u>, and <u>them</u>. EXAMPLE: Nanabush amazed **them**.

- **Write <u>S</u> if the underlined pronoun is used as a subject. Write <u>O</u> if it is used as an object.**

_____ 1. <u>We</u> read about Nanabush.

_____ 2. Wolf left <u>him</u> alone in the forest.

_____ 3. <u>She</u> told the tale in a whisper.

_____ 4. The story kept <u>us</u> guessing.

_____ 5. <u>It</u> was a real adventure.

_____ 6. Nanabush's cleverness surprised <u>us</u>.

- **Rewrite the sentences using a pronoun from the box in place of the underlined words.**

He   them   us   We

1. <u>Jesse and I</u> went to the rodeo.

_____

2. The friendly cowhand roped <u>two calves</u>.

_____

3. <u>The man</u> couldn't believe her strength.

_____

4. The cowhand gave <u>Jesse and me</u> a smile when she won.

_____

adjectives

> ■ A **possessive pronoun** is a pronoun that shows who
> or what owns something. The pronouns <u>my</u>, <u>our</u>, <u>your</u>,
> <u>his</u>, <u>her</u>, <u>its</u>, and <u>their</u> are possessive pronouns.
> EXAMPLE: Janet rode **her** bike to school.

■ **Underline the possessive pronoun in each sentence.**

1. Two monkeys did tricks for their trainers.

2. My family watched the monkeys.

3. Their names were Peg and Mike.

4. Peg tried to eat our lunch.

5. Then she put on her hat.

6. Mike clapped his hands.

■ **Write the correct possessive pronoun in each blank.**

1. Kieran lives in a house. _____ house is white.

2. I live in an apartment. _____ apartment has
   two bedrooms.

3. Tatiana lives on a farm. _____ farm is very big.

4. During the summer, Tom and Donna live on a houseboat.

   _____ houseboat goes up and down the river.

5. My family has one car. _____ car is old.

6. You have a new bike. _____ bike is blue and white.

7. The tree is big. _____ branches are long and thick.

8. Brian has a little brother. _____ brother's
   name is Robert.

Lesson 34
Using *I* or *Me*

- Use <u>I</u> in the subject of a sentence.
  EXAMPLE: **I** took Sara skating.
- Use <u>me</u> in the predicate of a sentence.
  EXAMPLE: Bev was waiting for **me**.
- Use <u>I</u> or <u>me</u> last when naming yourself and others.
  EXAMPLES: Juana and **I** like skating.
  Bev saw Marc and **me**.

■ **Complete the sentences with the words in ( ).**
Be sure to put the words in the correct order.

1. _____ and _____ wanted to go skating. (Liz, I)

2. Some of our friends were waiting for _____ and _____ . (me, her)

3. Anita went with _____ and _____ . (me, Liz)

4. _____ and _____ had a great time. (Liz, I)

5. _____ and _____ helped our friend Karen learn to skate. (I, Anita)

6. _____ and _____ held Karen's arms until she got to the rail. (I, Anita)

7. Karen smiled at _____ and _____ . (me, Anita)

8. Then _____ and _____ gave Karen a little push to get her started. (I, Anita)

9. Karen thanked _____ and _____ for helping her learn to skate. (me, Anita)

10. _____ and _____ were happy about that! (I, Anita)

© 1997 Gage Educational Publishing Company   Unit 3, Grammar and Usage

> ■ An **adjective** is a word that describes a noun or a pronoun. It tells which one, how many, or what kind.
> EXAMPLE: The **two** clocks made a **loud** ring.

■ **Underline the adjectives.**

1. The bright sunlight peeked through the window.

2. The noisy alarm woke me up.

3. It was a great day for the carnival.

4. I threw on my old clothes.

5. Three friends met me at school.

6. Funny clowns walked in the yard.

■ **Complete the sentences with adjectives from the list.**

big	empty	little	top
brown	first	muddy	white
cold	gold	new	clean
deep	happy	red	old

1. Ron won a _____ bear and a _____ cat.

2. Ann won a _____ tank with _____ fish in it.

3. The _____ girl chose a prize on the _____ shelf.

4. A balloon had a _____ bird and a _____ dog on it.

- Add -er to most adjectives to compare two persons, places, or things.

  EXAMPLE: The rabbit was **smaller** than the hat.

- Add -est to most adjectives to compare more than two persons, places, or things.

  EXAMPLE: That is the **smallest** rabbit I've seen.

■ **Underline the correct form of the adjective in each sentence.**

1. The magician's show was (longer, longest) than the clown's.

2. The clown's shoes were the (funnier, funniest) of all the shoes.

3. The stage was the (bigger, biggest) one I've ever seen.

4. Our laughs were the (louder, loudest) in the crowd.

5. Our seats were the (closer, closest) to the stage.

6. The tightrope was (higher, highest) than a building.

■ **Add -er or -est to the underlined adjective. Write the new words.**

1. The hand is <u>quick</u> than the eye. _____

2. That magician is the <u>great</u> in the world. _____

3. This is the <u>proud</u> moment of his life. _____

4. The white bird is <u>light</u> than the rabbit. _____

5. The rabbit is <u>soft</u> than the bird. _____

6. That trick is <u>old</u> than this country. _____

Using *A* or *An*

- Use <u>a</u> before words that begin with a consonant sound.   EXAMPLES: a child, a fresh egg
- Use <u>an</u> before words that begin with a vowel sound.   EXAMPLES: an adult, an old egg

- **Write <u>a</u> or <u>an</u>.**

1. _____ barn

2. _____ apple

3. _____ doctor

4. _____ test

5. _____ adventure

6. _____ balloon

7. _____ animal

8. _____ bedroom

9. _____ door

10. _____ house

11. _____ old barn

12. _____ red apple

13. _____ good doctor

14. _____ easy test

15. _____ happy adventure

16. _____ orange balloon

17. _____ clown's act

18. _____ upstairs room

19. _____ open door

20. _____ old house

- **Write <u>a</u> or <u>an</u> to complete this poem.**

The elephant didn't see –

_____ cat,

_____ ostrich,

_____ owl,

or a lion!

It saw another elephant!

- An **adverb** is a word that describes a verb. It tells
  how, when, or where. Many adverbs end in <u>ly</u>.
  EXAMPLES: The pig walked **slowly**. **How?**
  The pig walked **today**. **When?**
  The pig walked **there**. **Where?**

carefully
early   everywhere
far   happily   here
later   now   quickly,
quietly   then   out

- **The words above are adverbs. Write each word
  under aheading below to show if the word tells
  how, when, or where.**

HOW?	WHEN?	WHERE?
_____	_____	_____
_____	_____	_____
_____	_____	_____
_____		

- **Underline each adverb. Write <u>how</u>, <u>when</u>, or <u>where</u>.**

1. Shawn eats breakfast early.   _____

2. Andy walked quietly.   _____

3. We will eat later.   _____

4. The bird flew there.   _____

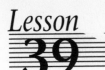

> ■ Use the adjective <u>good</u> to mean "better than average."
>   EXAMPLE: We had a **good** time.
> ■ Use the adverb <u>well</u> to mean "in a good way."
>   EXAMPLE: No one slept very **well**.

■ **Write <u>good</u> or <u>well</u>.**

1. We saw a _____ movie at the sleepover.

2. Carmen danced very _____ .

3. Everyone had a _____ time.

4. Lisa knows how to bake quite _____ .

5. She made a _____ pizza for us.

■ **Use <u>good</u> or <u>well</u> correctly in these paragraphs.**

Ben did not have a _____ time when he was ill.

But the doctor did his job _____ , so soon Ben

was able to go outside. He went to a _____ beach

to swim.

His _____ friend Marty went with him. Marty could

swim very _____ . They played on the beach and

made a _____ sandcastle. It was a _____

day for swimming.

Ben and Marty get along _____ and always

have a _____ time together.

- **Underline the singular nouns. Circle the plural nouns.**

    1. The garden will be full of flowers.

    2. The children will mow the yard.

    3. The roses are in the sun.

    4. The birds love the birdbath.

- **Underline the common nouns. Circle the proper nouns.**

    1. Greg bought seeds at Plant World.

    2. Greg scattered the seeds.

    3. He waters his plants every Monday.

    4. He'll have corn in July.

- **Underline the action verb. Circle the linking verbs. Write present or past on the lines.**

    1. The daisies grow quickly. _____

    2. The roses were droopy. _____

    3. The pansies are colourful. _____

- **Underline the correct verb.**

    1. A bee (rests, rest) in a flower.

    2. I (am, is, are) happy about the garden.

    3. It (were, was) raining yesterday.

    4. I (sees, see, seen) some new flowers.

    5. A garden (do, done, does) take time to grow.

    6. I (gone, goes, go) to the garden every day.

- **Underline the correct helping verb.**

    1. The family (has, have) moved.

    2. Dad (have, has) started his new job.

    3. The children (has, have) made some new friends.

- **Underline the correct pronoun.**

  1. (She, Her) took a break.

  2. This is (her, she) sandwich.

  3. Mary and (I, me) climbed a tree.

  4. We were in (we, our) yard.

  5. It is (me, my) birthday.

  6. Did you invite (their, them) to the party?

- **Underline each adjective that compares.**

  1. This leaf is the darkest on the twig.

  2. The twig is shorter than the branch.

  3. Can you reach the lowest branch?

  4. Your dog is older than my dog.

  5. My dog is faster than your dog.

  6. Our dogs are the greatest in the world.

- **Underline the adverbs.**

  1. The carrots grew quickly.

  2. The rain is falling softly.

  3. We'll have blossoms soon.

  4. The sun shines brightly.

  5. Winter came early this year.

  6. The soil is very rich.

- **Write good or well.**

  1. Dan slept _____ .

  2. He ate a _____ breakfast.

  3. Dan has studied _____ .

  4. He did _____ on his test.

  5. He got a _____ grade.

  6. Dan had a _____ day.

■ **The underlined words in the paragraph below are wrong. Rewrite the paragraph correctly.**

Monster Mack is looking at himself in the mirror.
Her hair look like dry grass. It need to be cut.
Our brown eyes flash and sparkles in the bright
light. The smile on his face are like a half moon.
It disappear when you see his nose. His nose is
smallest than his ears. It are good that her ears
are huge, though. Them get everyone's attention
when he wiggle they.

_____

_____

_____

_____

_____

_____

_____

_____

_____

_____

_____

- **Write a funny paragraph describing another monster.
  Then go back and circle two singular or plural
  nouns, two common or proper nouns, an action
  verb, a helping verb, two pronouns, three adjectives,
  and two adverbs. If you don't have all of these,
  add them to your paragraph.**

_____

_____

_____

_____

_____

_____

_____

_____

_____

_____

_____

_____

_____

_____

Lesson 40

Capitalizing Days, Holidays, and Months

> - Use a **capital letter** to begin proper nouns, such as days of the week, months, or holidays.
>   EXAMPLES: Monday, Friday, February, May, Thanksgiving, Canada Day
> - Use a **small letter** to begin the name of each season.
>   EXAMPLES: spring, summer, fall, winter

■ **Rewrite the words. Use capital letters where they are needed.**

1. mother's day _____

2. winter _____

3. july _____

4. saturday _____

5. june _____

6. spring _____

7. thursday _____

8. april _____

■ **Rewrite the sentences. Use capital letters where they are needed.**

1. This winter I am going to a party on valentine's day.

_____

_____

2. The party is in february.

_____

3. It is on saturday.

_____

4. Last summer I went to a parade on labour day.

_____

_____

Unit 4, Capitalization and Punctuation

> ■ Use a capital letter to begin each word in proper
> nouns, such as names of people, family names, and
> place names.
>> EXAMPLES: Gary Woodlawn, Grandma Cary, London,
>> British Columbia
> ■ Use a small letter to begin a family name that comes
> after words like <u>my</u>, <u>your</u>, and <u>their</u>.
>> EXAMPLES: their uncle, my grandma

■ **Rewrite the words. Use capital letters where they are needed.**

1. uncle brian _____

2. yellowknife _____

3. jamie smith _____

4. my grandfather _____

5. north bay _____

6. manitoba _____

7. aunt sue _____

8. charles _____

9. france _____

10. montréal _____

■ **Rewrite the sentences. Use capital letters where they are needed.**

1. We put on a play about ramona quimby.

_____

2. Did your uncle from red deer see it?

_____

3. I think aunt marta liked it.

_____

4. susan allen had the part of ramona.

> ■ Use a capital letter to begin the first word of a
>   sentence.   EXAMPLE: The pony licked her hand.

■ **Write the sentences. Use a capital letter to begin each sentence.**

1. would you like to have a pony?

    _____

2. elena has a pretty red pony.

    _____

3. her pony's name is Rosie.

    _____

4. she rides her pony every day.

    _____

5. it is tiny, but fast.

    _____

6. the pony races through the fields.

    _____

7. elena brushes her pony.

    _____

8. then it takes a nap.

    _____

9. a pony is a fun pet.

    _____

> - Use a **period** (.) at the end of a sentence that tells something.
>   - EXAMPLE: Ron has a new guppy.
> - Use a **question mark** (?) at the end of a sentence that asks a question.
>   - EXAMPLE: Did he name it?
> - Use an **exclamation point** (!) at the end of a sentence that shows strong feelings.
>   - EXAMPLE: What a good swimmer it is!

- **Use a period, question mark, or exclamation point at the end of each sentence.**

  1. Guppies can live in a large bowl of water
  2. Does the water need to be cleaned
  3. Look at the pretty colours
  4. Can you count how many there are
  5. What a long tail that guppy has

- **Write the sentences. End each one with a period, question mark, or exclamation point.**

  1. Do you feed guppies dry food

     _____

  2. I can't believe how well they swim

     _____

  3. The biggest guppy is named Butch

     _____

  4. What is the little one's name

     _____

  5. I like him the best

     _____

Lesson 44

> ■ An **abbreviation** is the shortened form of a word.
> ■ Use a capital letter to begin an abbreviation for a title of respect or an abbreviation for the name of a place. Use a period at the end of these abbreviations.
> > EXAMPLES: Ms., Mrs., Mr., Dr., Yellow Brick Rd.
> ■ An **initial** is the first letter of a name. Capitalize an initial and put a period after it.
> > EXAMPLE: L. M. Montgomery for Lucy Maude Montgomery

■ **Write the names. Correct the initials and the abbreviations that are underlined. Use capital letters and periods where they are needed.**

1. Laura i Wilder _____

2. mrs Tolan _____

3. Cherry Tree rd _____

4. dr Doolittle _____

5. a a Milne _____

6. ms t Lowry _____

7. Quimby st _____

8. mrs Banks _____

9. e m Thomas _____

■ **Circle the mistakes in the sentence below. Write each correction on a line.**

ms Binney is in a book by b Cleary.

1. _____   2. _____

Lesson 45

Abbreviating Names of Days and Months

- Use capital letters to begin abbreviations for days of the week. Use periods at the end of the abbreviations.
  EXAMPLES: Sun., Mon., Wed., Thurs., Sat.
- Use capital letters to begin abbreviations for months of the year. Use periods at the end of abbreviations.
  EXAMPLES: Jan., Feb., Apr., Aug., Nov., Dec.

- **Write the abbreviations for the days and the months. Use capital letters and periods where they are needed.**

1. Thursday _____
2. August _____
3. Sunday _____
4. March _____
5. Tuesday _____
6. February _____
7. Monday _____
8. September _____

9. October _____
10. Saturday _____
11. December _____
12. Wednesday _____
13. November _____
14. Friday _____
15. January _____
16. April _____

- **Circle the mistakes in the sentences below. Write each correction on a line.**

1. Tran asked me to a party on sat, sept 4th.

_____   _____

2. I'm having a party on fri, oct 31st.

_____   _____

- Use a **comma** (,) after the words <u>yes</u> and <u>no</u> if they begin a sentence.   EXAMPLES: Yes, I saw the clowns at the parade. No, I didn't see them dance.
- Use a comma to separate three or more items listed together in a sentence.   EXAMPLE: The float was red, white, and blue.

- **Write the sentences. Use commas where they are needed.**

1. Yes the band was in the parade.

   _____

2. Patty Carlos and Jo rode on a float.

   _____

3. We saw the bands clowns and floats.

   _____

4. Horses fire engines and flags came next.

   _____

5. No I didn't stay until the end.

   _____

6. Yes I wanted to stay.

   _____

7. We bought juice nuts and fruit to eat.

   _____

8. Yes I waved to the woman on the horse.

   _____

9. No she didn't see me.

   _____

Writing Letters Correctly

- Use a comma between numbers for the day and year in the **heading** of a letter. EXAMPLE: June 26, 1997
- Use a comma between the city and province in an **address.** Use capital letters in the postal code.
    EXAMPLE: Carstairs, Alberta T0M 0N1
- Use a capital letter to begin the first word and all names in the **greeting** of a letter. Use a comma at the end of the greeting. EXAMPLE: Dear Mom,
- Use a capital letter to begin only the first word in the **closing** of a letter. Use a comma at the end of the closing. EXAMPLE: Very truly yours,

- **Circle the words that should be capitalized in the letter. Add commas where needed.**

34 Duke Street
Dryden Ontario p8n 1c3
April 3 1997

dear gina

I'm really glad you got to come for a visit. I had a lot of fun. Please write soon.

your friend

Danielle

- **Rewrite these parts of a letter. Use capital letters and commas where they are needed.**

1. May 7 1997 _____

2. regina Saskatchewan s4x 1g8 _____

3. dear alicia _____ 4. with love _____

- Add an **apostrophe** (') and -<u>s</u> ('<u>s</u>) to nouns like <u>girl</u> to show that one person owns something.
  EXAMPLE: the **girl's** present
- Add an apostrophe after nouns like <u>girls</u> to show that more than one person owns something.
  EXAMPLE: the **girls'** presents
- Add an apostrophe and -<u>s</u> ('<u>s</u>) to plural nouns like <u>children</u> to show that more than one person owns something.   EXAMPLE: the **children's** presents

- **Rewrite each phrase to show ownership. Add an apostrophe or an apostrophe and -<u>s</u> to the underlined words.**

1. the <u>pilot</u> hat
_____

2. the <u>woman</u> car
_____

3. five <u>dogs</u> bones
_____

4. a <u>kittens</u> toys
_____

5. a <u>clown</u> hat
_____

6. many <u>mens</u> hats
_____

7. the <u>women</u> cars
_____

8. a <u>snowman</u> nose
_____

9. ten <u>kites</u> strings
_____

10. the <u>birds</u> nests
_____

- **Write a sentence telling about something that belongs to a friend or friends. Use an apostrophe or an apostrophe and -<u>s</u> to show who owns it.**

_____

_____

_____

Lesson
49

- A **contraction** is a word made by joining two words.
- Use an apostrophe to show that letters are left out.
  EXAMPLES: **it's** = it is **hasn't** = has not

- **Write contractions for the pairs of words.**
  Leave out the letters that are underlined.

  1. she + is _____

  2. we + are _____

  3. you + will _____

  4. I + have _____

  5. he + would _____

  6. she + has _____

- **Write contractions for the pairs of words.**

  1. has + not _____

  2. is + not _____

  3. were + not _____

  4. I + will _____

  5. that + is _____

  6. would + not _____

  7. they + will _____

  8. there + is _____

- **Rewrite the sentences. Use contractions for the**
  words that are underlined.

  1. Jay has not seen the movie.

  _____

  2. It is about a strange land.

  _____

  3. One year winter does not come.

  _____

  4. The people do not mind.

  _____

© 1997 Gage Educational Publishing Company **61**

Lesson 50

Using Quotation Marks

- Use **quotation marks** (" ") before and after the words a speaker says.   EXAMPLE: Mother said, "I'm going to leave for about an hour."
- Use a comma between the words the speaker says and the rest of the sentence. Put the comma before the quotation marks. Capitalize the first word the speaker says.   EXAMPLES: "We're leaving now," said Mother. **or** Mother said, "We're leaving now."

- **Read the cartoon. Think about who is talking and what they are saying.**

- **Answer the questions about the cartoon. Use quotation marks and commas where needed.**

1. What did Carl say first?

   "Yes, Mother," said Carl. **or** Carl said, "Yes, Mother."

2. What did Jane say first?

   _____

3. What did Jane say about the butter?

   _____

4. What was the last thing Carl said?

   _____

- **Correct the sentences. Circle letters that should be capitalized. Put periods, question marks, exclamation points, and commas where they are needed.**

    1. mr and mrs kamp lived in a house on may street

    2. one Saturday the family cleaned the attic

    3. ellen found an old letter from dr r m wilson

    4. the letter came all the way from japan

    5. we found a picture of roses daisies and tulips

    6. did dad take that photo on valentine's day

    7. no my aunt took the photo last april

    8. what a mess the attic is

    9. yes mom will clean out the attic next spring

    10. ellen jason and beth will help mom

- **Rewrite the abbreviations. Use capital letters and periods where needed.**

    1. tues _____

    2. fri _____

    3. mrs _____

    4. elm st _____

    5. dec _____

    6. m c lee _____

    7. apr _____

    8. j r adams _____

    9. feb _____

    10. mon _____

    11. smith rd _____

    12. mr _____

    13. sat _____

    14. dr a roberts _____

    15. ms n Lincoln _____

    16. aug _____

- **Add commas to these parts of a letter. Circle the small letters that should be capital letters.**

1. kelowna british columbia v1y 3b2

2. august 18 1997

3. dear kim

4. yours truly

5. dear mom

6. toronto ontario m1c 4j3

7. sincerely

8. dear dr. west

9. your friend

10. dec. 1 1997

11. montréal québec h3s 1g1

12. with love

- **Add apostrophes, quotation marks, and commas to these sentences where they are needed.**

1. This is Ellens game said Indira.

2. Tom said Its her favourite.

3. Id like to play said Mike.

4. Mike Indira and Nancy sat down to play.

5. It isnt hard to play Tom said.

6. Lets read the rules together said Indira.

7. The games rules are printed on the box said Mike.

8. Were ready to begin playing said Indira.

9. Mike said Ill go first.

10. Its Nancys turn to go first said Indira.

11. Nancy doesnt want to play.

12. Shed rather read Ellens book.

■ **Correct the story. As you read it, circle letters that should be capitals. Put periods, question marks, exclamation points, commas, apostrophes, and quotation marks where they are needed. Rewrite the title and the story on the lines.**

<u>A Hidden Surprise</u>

gina's cat is named sam_____ what a big smart

beautiful cat he is_____ one summer day, gina couldnt

find him_____ do you know where he was_____

he was under the porch with three new kittens_____

gina said your name is samantha now_____

_____

_____

_____

_____

_____

_____

_____

_____

_____

- **Write a letter to Gina. Tell her what you think about her surprise. Use your address and today's date in the heading. Write a greeting and a closing. Be sure to use an abbreviation and a contraction in your letter. Use capital letters, periods, question marks, exclamation points, commas, and apostrophes. Check your letter for any mistakes.**

_____

_____

_____

_____

_____

_____

_____

_____

_____

_____

_____

_____

_____

_____

_____

_____

_____

    Unit 4, Capitalization and Punctuation

- A **sentence** must tell a complete thought.
- Remember to begin a sentence with a capital letter and end it with a period, a question mark, or an exclamation point.
  EXAMPLE: **Thought**: making our puppets
  Sentence: We are making puppets.

- **Write each of these thoughts about making a puppet as a sentence.**

1. finding some yarn for our puppet's hair

   _____

2. cutting yarn for the puppet's hair

   _____

3. gluing the yarn to our puppet's head

   _____

4. making a face on the puppet's head

   _____

5. making a costume for our puppet

   _____

6. sewing buttons on the costume

   _____

7. dressing the puppet

   _____

8. putting shoes on the puppet

   _____

9. using the puppet in a puppet show

   _____

- A **paragraph** is a group of sentences about one main idea. **Indent** the first line. To indent a paragraph, leave a space before the first word.
- A paragraph should have sentences about the same subject.

  EXAMPLE:

  Last night my brother and I put on a puppet show. We invited our parents and our little sister, Becky. Dad made popcorn, and everyone laughed.

- **Read the paragraph. Then write another paragraph. Tell what else you think happened in this puppet show. Be sure to indent.**

  My brother's puppet was named Morris. My puppet was Garfield. Morris was a fussy cat, and Garfield was his funny friend. Morris wouldn't eat much. Garfield loved to eat. Garfield asked my family to share their popcorn with him. Everyone agreed to share.

_____

_____

_____

_____

_____

_____

_____

- A **topic sentence** tells the main idea, or topic, of a paragraph.
- All sentences in a paragraph should be about that topic.

    EXAMPLE: <u>Liquid soap bottles make wonderful hand puppets</u>. Just turn the bottle upside down, and paint a face on the bottom part. If you wish, glue a piece of cloth around the middle of the bottle. Stick your finger in the top of the bottle. There's your puppet!

- **Underline the topic sentence in each paragraph.**

Many people are needed to put on a puppet show. Someone must make the puppets and the set. Others must move the puppets and act in the show. Someone is needed to seat people and dim the lights.

_____

Shadow puppets are different from other kinds of puppets. You look at the shadow of the puppet instead of the puppet. The puppets are held and moved in front of a light so their shadows look alive.

_____

The person holding the puppet makes the puppet move. Some puppets move by strings that can be pulled. Others fit over a hand and move when the hand moves. Some puppets seem to talk when they are held the right way.

> ■ **Details** after the topic sentence in a paragraph should tell more about the main idea.
>
> EXAMPLE: Liquid soap bottles make wonderful hand puppets. Just turn the bottle upside down, and paint a face on the bottom part. If you wish, glue a piece of cloth around the middle of the bottle. Stick your finger in the top of the bottle. There's your puppet!

■ **Circle the topic sentence. Underline the four sentences that give details about the main idea. Write the circled and underlined sentences in a new paragraph.**

Our puppet show was a great success. Parents, friends, and neighbours came to see it. I am going to learn how to swim this summer. Altogether, we sold twenty tickets and made $10.00. Rita already knows how to swim. Everyone liked the show and clapped for about two minutes after it was over. My uncle's name is Tony. He knows how to swim well. A good time was had by all!

_____

_____

_____

_____

Lesson 55

- The details in a paragraph can be arranged in different ways. One way to arrange details is to put them in the **order** in which they happen.
- Words such as <u>first</u>, <u>next</u>, <u>then</u>, and <u>finally</u> help to show order.

  EXAMPLE: To make a ball-and-pencil puppet, **first** punch a sharp pencil into a soft ball. **Next**, wrap a piece of cloth just under the ball. **Then** tie a ribbon around the top part of the cloth. **Finally**, glue yarn hair on the ball and draw a face with markers.

- **Write numbers to show the right order in the paragraphs.**

_____ Next, give the people a program that lists the puppet characters. _____ Finally, call out, "Let the show begin!" _____ First, collect the tickets on the night of the big show._____ Then, when everyone is seated, dim the lights. _____ Help people find their seats in the audience.

_____

_____ Next, the piano music started. _____ Then two puppets, a clown, and a donkey sang to the music. _____ Finally, the curtain came down. _____ First, the curtain went up. _____ Everyone laughed and clapped when the donkey sang "Hee-Haw."

- **Purpose** in writing is the reason why something is written.
- One purpose is to tell about a thought or feeling.
  EXAMPLE: I thought I'd never stop laughing.
- Another purpose is to describe something.
  EXAMPLE: The bright red colour of the bird shone through the waving branches of the trees.
- Another purpose is to give information.
  EXAMPLE: The science fair is today.
- Another purpose is to tell about something that is make-believe.
  EXAMPLE: The snowflakes talked to one another as they fell to the ground.

- **Write a sentence that tells how you feel about going to puppet shows.**

_____

- **Write a sentence that describes a puppet.**

_____

_____

- **Write a sentence that gives some information about a puppet show.**

_____

_____

- **Write the first sentence of a make-believe story that could be used for a puppet show.**

_____

_____

Choosing a Topic

> Here are some steps to follow in choosing a **topic**.
> - Write a list of persons, things, or animals that interest you. Then circle the topic that especially interests you.
>   - EXAMPLES: clowns, (putting on a puppet show), tigers
> - Divide the topic into smaller parts. Choose the one that you would like to write about.
>   - EXAMPLES: making a princess puppet, sending out invitations, practising for the show

- **You are going to write a paragraph. Your purpose is to give someone information about how to make something. You need to choose a topic. Write a list of different things you can make.**

1. _____

2. _____

3. _____

4. _____

5. _____

6. _____

- **Circle the topic that especially interests you.**

- **Divide the topic you circled into smaller parts. Underline the one you would like to write about.**

1. _____	4. _____
2. _____	5. _____
3. _____	6. _____

How-to Paragraph

- The purpose of some paragraphs is to give instructions.
- A **how-to paragraph** tells how to do something.

  EXAMPLE:

  How to Make a Soap-Bottle King Puppet

  It is not hard to make a soap-bottle king puppet. To begin, search through your house for materials to make your puppet. You will need to find a dishwashing soap bottle, scrap cloth, paper, and markers. First, make the puppet head by turning the bottle upside down. Draw a face and hair on the bottle with markers. Next, glue a paper crown above the face. Then glue a piece of scrap cloth around the middle of the bottle. Put your finger in the opening of the bottle, and say "Hello" to the king.

- **Write the topic sentence for the paragraph in the box.**

_____

- **Write four sentences that give details about the topic.**

_____

_____

_____

_____

_____

_____

- **Look at the topic you chose on page 73. Write a how-to paragraph about your topic. Use the model on page 74 to help you. Be sure to include a good topic sentence and the steps you would follow.**

_____

_____

_____

_____

_____

_____

_____

_____

_____

_____

_____

_____

_____

_____

- An **invitation** is a kind of letter. An invitation tells the following things: **who** will give the event, **what** kind of event it will be, **when** it will begin and end, and **where** it will take place.
- An invitation includes the address or telephone number of the sender.

EXAMPLE:

569 North Street
Guelph, Ontario
N1H 4C9
August 6, 19____

Dear Selim,
    Please come to a puppet show on Saturday, August 20. It will be at Mary Baldwin's house, 22 Oak Avenue, from 3:00 to 4:00. See you then!
                Your neighbour,
Call 555-6340   Craig

- **Write an invitation to a party you would like to have.**

_____

_____

_____

_____

_____

_____

_____

_____

- A **telephone message** tells:
  1. The **day** and **time** the message was received.
  2. The **name** of the person getting the message.
  3. The **name** of the person who called.
  4. The **phone number** of the person who called.
  5. The important **information** from the call.
  6. The **name** of the person who took the message.

  EXAMPLE: 97/04/18
                                             10:15 a.m.

  Jay—
     Beth Bishop called and wants you to call her
  back at 555-3958. She needs to ask you how to
  make soap-bottle puppets for her play.
                                             Megan

- **Read this part of a telephone call. Then write the message Henry might leave for Terry. Write today's date and time.**

HENRY: "Terry isn't home. I'll take a message for him."

MAYA: "Please tell him to call me back at 555-2749.
         I want him to get some cloth for the puppets
         we're making. Thanks. Goodbye."

(Date) _____

(Time) _____

(To) _____

(Message) _____

_____

(From) _____

■ **Write each thought as a sentence.**

1. putting the puppet on my hand

_____

2. making the puppet nod its head

_____

3. moving the puppet's mouth

_____

■ **Circle the topic sentence in the paragraph below.
Then underline only the sentences that give
details about the main idea.**

A break between acts in a play is needed. It allows

time for the crowd to get up and stretch. Amina is a

very good math student. It lets the people in the show

get ready for the rest of the play. It also gives time to

prepare for the next act.

■ **Write numbers to show the correct order of the details for
each set of directions below.**

_____ Then let the popcorn pop. _____ First, pour

popcorn into a pan. _____ Finally, serve it to the crowd.

_____ Next, put a lid on top of the pan.

_____

_____ Then mix the juice and water together. _____ Finally,

pour the juice into glasses. _____ First, spoon frozen

juice into a pitcher. _____ Next, add cold water.

- **Write a sentence that tells how you feel about owning a pet.**

  _____

- **Write a sentence that describes a pet you own or would like to own.**

  _____

  _____

- **Write a sentence that gives some information about how to care for a pet.**

  _____

  _____

- **Write the first sentence of a make-believe story about a magical pet.**

  _____

- **Write an invitation to a picnic that your class is having.**

  _____

  _____

  _____

  _____

  _____

  _____

  _____

- **Read this story.**

> One day Sam was looking for something fun to do. Sam decided he would like to ask his friend Hoan to come over to play. Sam's mother said that he should call Hoan after lunch. Sam was so excited, thinking about all the fun they'd have together. Since it was such a nice day, they would be able to play outside. Sam decided to ask Hoan to bring his bike so that they could ride together.

- **Pretend that Hoan is not home when Sam calls. Write a telephone message for Hoan. Write the important information from the call. Use the correct names, today's date, the time, and your phone number.**

_____

_____

_____

_____

_____

_____

_____

_____

_____

- **Write an invitation to a show that your class might put on.**

_____

_____

_____

_____

_____

_____

_____

- **Write a how-to paragraph telling how to get to your house. Write a topic sentence and supporting details. Use words such as <u>first</u>, <u>next</u>, and <u>then</u> to put the details in order.**

_____

_____

_____

_____

_____

_____

_____

- **Directions** must be followed step-by-step.
- Sometimes maps help you to follow directions. They might show which way is north, south, east, and west by the letters <u>N</u>, <u>S</u>, <u>E</u>, and <u>W</u>.

EXAMPLE:

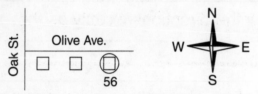

Directions to Adele's House

1) Go north on Oak Street.
2) Turn east on Olive Avenue.
3) Walk down 3 houses to 56 Olive Avenue.

- **Look at the map, and read the directions to Joseph's house. Then answer the questions.**

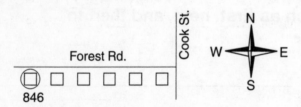

1) Go south on Cook Street.
2) Turn west on Forest Road.
3) Walk down 6 houses to 846 Forest Road.

1. What direction should you go first? _____

2. What street should you walk on first? _____

3. What direction should you go next? _____

4. What street would you be on?_____

5. How many houses down Forest Road is Joseph's house? _____

- Carefully read everything before beginning to follow written directions.
- Pay close attention to words that tell the order of the steps you must follow.

  EXAMPLES: first, second, next, later, then, now, finally
- Be sure to follow the directions exactly as they are written.

■ **Read the recipe shown below. Then answer the questions.**

Chocolate Banana Pops

First, remove the banana peel, and cut the banana into four pieces. Next, push a popsicle stick into the centre of each piece. Then put the banana pops on a cookie sheet and freeze them. Melt 125 mL chocolate chips and 30 mL margarine over low heat. Dip the frozen bananas in the chocolate. Place the chocolate-covered bananas on a cookie sheet covered with waxed paper, and place them in the freezer.

1. What tools do you need for this recipe? _____

_____

2. What ingredients do you need? _____

_____

3. What should you do just before you freeze the banana pops for the first

time? _____

_____

4. What is the last thing you do to complete the recipe? _____

_____

> ■ Things that are alike in some way can be **grouped** together. The name of the group tells how the things in the group are alike.
> EXAMPLE: Dogs, cats, and horses are all animals.

■ **Underline the words that belong in each group.**

1. **animals**   sand   mouse   monkey   sheep   flower   bird
2. **foods**   bread   hat   egg   carrot   apple   fish
3. **colours**   blue   red   grass   purple   orange   cow
4. **fruits**   apple   cake   orange   milk   banana   grape
5. **clothes**   pants   foot   shirt   jacket   pale   hat
6. **round things**   ball   desk   circle   rake   penny   orange
7. **flying things**   bike   bird   jet   snake   rocket   turtle
8. **boys' names**   Peter   Ann   Mike   Jill   Josh   Tom
9. **girls' names**   Karen   David   Pam   Bill   Elaine   Melanie
10. **vegetables**   peas   apples   carrots   beans   corn   tuna
11. **tools**   hammer   saw   chair   shovel   rake   desk

■ **Write the words below under the correct heading.**

monkey	school	potato
carrot	elephant	store
house	corn	lion

Zoo Animals   **Vegetables**   **Buildings**

_____   _____   _____

_____   _____   _____

_____   _____   _____

> - The **table of contents** is in the front of a book. It lists titles and page numbers of parts of the book.
>   EXAMPLE:
>   Synonyms 1
>   Antonyms 2
>   Homonyms 3
>   More Homonyms 4
>   Words with More Than One Meaning 5

- **Use the table of contents in this book to answer the questions.**

1. How many units are in this book? _____

2. What is the title of Unit 5? _____

3. On what page is "Using Commas in Sentences" in Unit 4? _____

4. What is the title of page 14? _____

5. On what page is "Writing Sentences" in Unit 5? _____

6. What is the title of page 48? _____

7. Which unit would help you learn more about grammar and usage? _____

8. On what page does Unit 6 begin? _____

9. On what page is "Compound Words" in Unit 1? _____

10. On what page does Unit 1 end? _____

11. On what page does the Unit 1 Final Review begin? _____

12. On what page does the Unit 5 Final Review end? _____

13. On what page is "Sentences" in Unit 2? _____

14. Which unit would help you learn more about vocabulary? _____

Using an Index

> ■ An **index** is in the back of a book. It lists the subjects of the book in alphabetical order and gives page numbers.
>
> EXAMPLE:
>
> Abbreviations, 56, 57, 63, 66, 102, 103
> Adjectives
>   definition of, 43
>   identifying, 43, 44, 47, 51, 101
>   that compare, 44, 49, 50, 101
>   that describe, 43, 101

■ **Use the index of this book to answer the questions.**

1. On what page is the index of this book? _____

2. What pages tell about suffixes? _____

3. What pages tell about antonyms? _____

4. What pages tell about quotation marks? _____

5. Are the words <u>business letters</u> listed in the index? _____

6. What pages tell about action verbs? _____

7. Under which heading should you look if you want to learn about homographs? _____

8. What are three examples of specific punctuation marks listed in the index? _____

9. Under which heading do you find letter writing? _____

10. What pages tell about telephone messages? _____

- **Alphabetical order** is the order of the letters in the alphabet. To put words in alphabetical order, look at the first letter of each word. Use the first letter of each word to put the words in the order of the alphabet.

   EXAMPLES: **b**ag, **p**ack, **c**ottage = **b**ag, **c**ottage, **p**ack

- Look at the second letter if the words begin with the same letter.

   EXAMPLES: **fi**sh, **fr**y, **fe**ast = **fe**ast, **fi**sh, **fr**y

- **Write each set of words in alphabetical order.**

oar canoe paddle		giant good glass
1. _____		1. _____
2. _____		2. _____
3. _____		3. _____

town week ranch		bounce ball beach
1. _____		1. _____
2. _____		2. _____
3. _____		3. _____

east soap dream		pole price pump
1. _____		1. _____
2. _____		2. _____
3. _____		3. _____

- **Guide words** are at the top of each dictionary page. They show the first and last words on the page. Every word listed on the page comes between the guide words.

  EXAMPLE: **oak / real**

  oak   〰〰〰
  ocean   ready
  〰〰〰   rea**l**

- **Write the pair of guide words that each word comes between.**

<table>
<tr><td align="center">**add / chase**</td><td align="center">**quack / weep**</td></tr>
<tr><td>1. beehive ___add / chase___</td><td>5. usual _____</td></tr>
<tr><td>2. reason _____</td><td>6. cabin _____</td></tr>
<tr><td>3. wall _____</td><td>7. quiet _____</td></tr>
<tr><td>4. attach _____</td><td>8. spark _____</td></tr>
</table>

- **Write the word that would be on the same page as each set of guide words.**

iron	across	ill	dine	dad	job
arrow	weight	ship	wonder	herd	post

1. idea / in _____	7. cut / desk _____
2. apple / axe _____	8. serve / space _____
3. different / dry _____	9. able / ago _____
4. jar / just _____	10. wheat / wrong _____
~ insect / island _____	11. hair / hose _____
~ wagon / winter _____	12. pine / price _____

1997 Gage Educational Publishing Company

Unit 6, Study Skills

- Words that are listed on a dictionary page are called **entry words**. They are listed in alphabetical order.
- A dictionary gives the **definition**, or meaning, for each entry word.
- Some words have more than one meaning. Then each meaning is numbered.

    EXAMPLE: **easy 1** not hard. **2** free from trouble.

calf 1 a young cow or bull. **2** the young of other animals.
call 1 speak loudly. **2** to give a name to. **3** to ring up on the telephone.

carol a song of joy.
carpet 1 a thick, heavy, woven covering for floors. **2** to cover with a carpet.

- **Read the definitions of each entry word. Then answer the questions.**

1. Which word has one meaning? _____

2. Which word has three meanings? _____

3. Which words have two meanings? _____

4. Which word means "a song"? _____

5. Write a sentence with one meaning of <u>carpet</u>. _____

   _____

6. Write a sentence with one meaning of <u>call</u>. _____

   _____

7. Write a sentence with the first meaning of <u>calf</u>. _____

   _____

part **1** something less than the whole.
  2 the line made when hair is combed.
  3 an actor's role.
pass 1 to go by. **2** to do the opposite
  of fail.
peace 1 freedom from war. **2** quiet.
pen 1 something to write with. **2** a place
  to keep animals.

place 1 space taken up by a person or
  thing. **2** a city, town, country, or other
  area. **3** to put.
plant 1 a living thing that is not an animal.
  2 to put something in the ground to grow.
point 1 a sharp end. **2** a method of
  scoring in a game. **3** the main idea or
  important part.

■ **The entry words in the box have more than one meaning. Write the number of the correct meaning next to each sentence.**

1. My old red <u>pen</u> ran out of ink. _____

2. Naomi couldn't find a <u>place</u> for her table. _____

3. They will <u>plant</u> daisies in the spring. _____

4. Arnold sat in the chair to get some <u>peace</u>. _____

5. Did most of the class <u>pass</u> the test? _____

6. Don't <u>place</u> the candles too near the heat. _____

7. What kind of <u>plant</u> are you growing? _____

8. The little pigs were in a <u>pen</u>. _____

9. Do you have to travel far to get to the <u>place</u>? _____

10. Did the car <u>pass</u> the truck? _____

11. Do the soldiers want <u>peace</u> or war? _____

12. Kirk scored ten <u>points</u> in basketball. _____

13. He only played for <u>part</u> of the game. _____

14. The teacher asks us to keep a <u>point</u> on our pencils. _____

15. Everyone had a <u>part</u> in our class play. _____

16. There was no <u>part</u> in her hair. _____

90

1997 Gage Educational Publishing Company

Unit 6, Study Skills

Lesson 70 — Dictionary: Pronunciation

- Each word listed in a dictionary is followed by a respelling of the word. The respelling shows how to **pronounce**, or say, the word. The respelling is in parentheses following the entry word.
- **Accent marks** show which word parts are said with the most force. EXAMPLES: sər prīz´ tē´ chər
- A **pronunciation key** (shown below) contains letters and special symbols, along with sample words, that show how the letters should be pronounced.

- **Use the pronunciation key to answer the following questions.**

1. What key word is given for u̇? _____

2. What key word is given for ô? _____

3. What key words are given for ə? _____
_____

> hat, āge, fär; let, ēqual, tėrm; it, īce; hot, ōpen, ôrder; oil, out; cup, pu̇t, rüle; əbove, takən, pencəl, lemən, circəs; ch, child; ng, long; sh, ship; th, thin; ᵀн, then; zh, measure

- **Study each respelling using the pronunciation key. Then circle the word that matches the respelling.**

1. (chōz)   shoes   chose   choice
2. (let'ər)   letter   lettuce   ladder
3. (sī'əns)   since   scenes   science
4. (kär'tən)   cartoon   carton   garden
5. (ᵀнēz)   these   this   those
6. (mezh'ər)   messier   messenger   measure
7. (fyü'əl)   fuel   full   file

- **Read the directions below. Then answer the questions.**

> You can make a boat from half of a walnut shell. First, carefully open the shell by cracking it where the two halves join. Second, remove the nut from the shell. Then place one end of a toothpick into one end of a shell half. Next, glue the toothpick to the shell. Cut a small sail from construction paper. Finally, glue the sail to the toothpick.

1. What can you make using these directions? _____

   _____

2. What should you do first? _____

   _____

3. What should you do after you glue the toothpick to the shell? _____

   _____

- **Circle the words that belong in each group.**

   1. **babies**   puppy   chick   cat   kitten   lamb   dog
   2. **seasons**   fall   day   spring   summer   rain   winter
   3. **fruit**   beans   apples   oranges   peas   pears   seeds

- **Write the name of the group for each set of words.**

   1. pants   dress   shirt   skirt   coat

   _____

   2. lunch   supper   breakfast   dinner

   _____

   3. red   green   yellow   blue   orange

   _____

■ **Write each list of words in alphabetical order.**

1. seen _____   2. blue _____   3. press _____

   lake _____   bee _____   plough _____

   cage _____   bat _____   puff _____

■ **Use the index in this book to answer the following questions.**

1. What page gives a definition of adverbs? _____

2. What pages tell about exclamation points? _____

3. What pages tell about homonyms? _____

■ **Read the dictionary entries for <u>stalk</u> and <u>stand</u>. Write the meaning that goes with each sentence below.**

> **stalk 1** the stem of a plant. **2** to hunt.
> **stand 1** to be on one's feet. **2** to put up with.

1. I watched the cat <u>stalk</u> the wind-up toy.

   _____

2. Let's <u>stand</u> up and stretch.

   _____

3. We put the <u>stalk</u> in water to keep the plant alive.

   _____

4. I can't <u>stand</u> the smell of onions.

   _____

■ **Study each respelling using the pronunciation key. Then circle the word that matches the respelling.**

> hat, āge, fär; let, ēqual, tėrm; it, īce; hot, ōpen, ôrder; oil, out; cup, pút, rüle; əbove, takən, pencəl, lemən, circəs; ch, child; ng, long; sh, ship; th, thin; ŦH, then; zh, measure

1. (of´əl)   official   awful   useful

2. (rīm)   rhyme   rim   room

3. (van)   vane   van   than

- Imagine you are going shopping in a grocery store. To make your shopping trip quicker and easier, put the food items on the shopping list below into the groups in which they belong.

Shopping List: canned soup, potatoes, bananas, frozen orange juice, lettuce, chicken, broccoli, hamburger, apples, bacon

Fruits	Canned Foods	Vegetables
_____	_____	_____
_____	_____	_____
_____	_____	_____

Frozen Foods	Meat
_____	_____
_____	_____
_____	_____

- Use the table of contents in this book to answer the following questions.

1. What is the title of page 25? _____

2. On what page is "Linking Verbs" in Unit 3? _____

3. On what page is "Guide Words" in Unit 6? _____

4. What is the title of the lesson on page 85? _____

5. How many pages are in Unit 1? _____

6. What is the title of Unit 2? _____

- **Follow the directions to Diane's house. Circle her house on the map.**

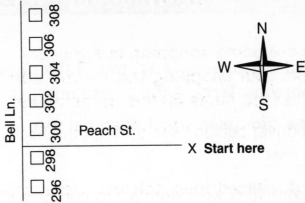

308
306
304
302
300   Peach St.
298
296

Bell Ln.

X **Start here**

1. Go west on Peach Street.

2. Turn north on Bell Lane.

3. Go down 5 houses to 308 Bell Lane.

- **Write directions to 296 Bell Lane.**

_____

_____

_____

- **Draw a map showing the street where you live. Draw a line to show what street crosses yours. Then write the directions to where you live.**

_____

_____

_____

Synonyms and Antonyms ▪ Write <u>S</u> if the underlined words are synonyms. Write <u>A</u> if they are antonyms.

_____ **1.** The driver couldn't see through the thick <u>fog</u> and <u>mist</u>.

_____ **2.** The gas tank went from <u>full</u> to <u>empty</u> in minutes.

_____ **3.** We couldn't see to our <u>right</u> or to our <u>left</u>.

_____ **4.** We had to <u>stop</u> on the side and wait for help because our car just wouldn't <u>go</u> anymore.

_____ **5.** When we stopped it was <u>light</u> outside, but now it is getting <u>dark</u>.

_____ **6.** We thought it would be a <u>short</u> wait, but no one came for a <u>long</u> time.

Homonyms ▪ Circle the correct homonym to complete each sentence.

1. Shanelle has been invited (two, to, too) a party.

2. Denise is going to the party, (too, to, two).

3. She asks Denise if the party starts at (to, too, two) o'clock.

4. Denise tells Shanelle that she needs to be (there, their, they're) at four o'clock.

5. The girls can hardly wait to (here, hear) that it is time for the party.

6. They plan to meet (here, hear) and go together.

96   **Vocabulary**

Words with More Than One Meaning ▪ Read the meanings in the box. Write the number of the meaning for each underlined word.

_____	**1.**	Tony turned on the <u>light</u> so he could see.
_____	**2.**	He picked up a <u>light</u> piece of wood.
_____	**3.**	It weighed less than one <u>pound</u>.
_____	**4.**	He used a special tool to <u>pound</u> a design into the wood.

> **pound 1** a weight equal to 454 grams **2** to hit hard over and over
> **light 1** not heavy **2** something by which we see

Prefixes ▪ Underline the prefix. Write the meaning of the word.

1. unable _____

2. relive _____

3. repay _____

Suffixes ▪ Underline the suffix. Write the meaning of the word.

1. worker _____

2. dryer _____

3. visitor _____

Compound Words and Contractions ▪ Make a compound word or a contraction from each pair of words. Circle the contractions.

1. some + one = _____

2. she + is = _____

3. I + will = _____

4. day + light = _____

Types of Sentences ▪ Write <u>S</u> for <u>statement</u>, <u>Q</u> for <u>question</u>, <u>C</u> for <u>command</u>, or <u>E</u> for <u>exclamation</u> for each sentence. Write <u>X</u> if the group of words is not a sentence.

_____ 1. Rob played basketball.

_____ 2. How many points did Park make?

_____ 3. What a good player she is!

_____ 4. Pass the ball to Lupe.

_____ 5. Scored ten points.

_____ 6. Which team do you think will win?

_____ 7. I hope Pat's team wins.

_____ 8. Both teams are doing a.

_____ 9. Lupe bounced the ball to Rob.

_____ 10. Shoot the ball, Rob.

Subjects and Predicates ▪ Underline each subject. Circle each predicate.

1. The new game began.

2. Jay quickly bounced the ball.

3. Vicki picked up the pass.

4. Todd blocked the shot.

5. Carl jumped for the ball.

6. The other team got the ball.

7. Lise tried to shoot a basket.

8. The ball bounced off the rim.

9. Vicki scored two points.

10. Everyone gave a loud cheer.

 Sentences

Combining Subjects and Predicates ■ Combine the sentences. Write the new sentences.

1. Dan signalled to Jack. Dan passed the ball.

    _____

2. Victor wanted to play. Tamara wanted to play.

    _____

3. They won today. They lost last week.

    _____

Writing Clear Sentences ■ Read the sentences. Write two sentences for each.

1. Mark enjoys all kinds of sports, his favourite sport is basketball.

    _____

    _____

2. Mark's mother used to play basketball, she was on a team in high school.

    _____

    _____

3. Mark finds a photo of his mother playing basketball, he shows it to his friend Tina.

    _____

    _____

4. Tina's mother is in the photo, her mother used to play basketball, too.

    _____

    _____

Singular and Plural Nouns ▪ Write <u>S</u> before each singular noun. Then write its plural form. Write <u>P</u> before each plural noun. Then write its singular form.

_____ 1. branches_____

_____ 2. toe_____

_____ 3. bus_____

_____ 4. boxes _____

_____ 5. cart _____

_____ 6. tigers _____

Proper and Common Nouns ▪ Write <u>P</u> before each proper noun. Then write a common noun for it. Write <u>C</u> before each common noun. Then write a proper noun for it.

_____ 1. friend _____

_____ 2. Alberta _____

_____ 3. school _____

_____ 4. Lake Erie _____

Verbs ▪ Underline each action verb. Circle each linking verb. Write <u>present</u> or <u>past</u>.

1. Katie lives in Calgary.   _____

2. I visited her in June.   _____

3. Diane was in Calgary last year.   _____

Using the Correct Verb ▪ Draw a line under the correct verb.

1. Joel (saw, seen) the train pulling out of the station.

2. He needed to (buy, buys) a ticket to Sudbury, Ontario.

3. Joel (runs, run) to catch the train.

4. He should (have, has) gotten there earlier.

5. Joel (were, was) waving to get the train to stop.

6. But the train (did, do) not stop.

Using the Correct Pronoun ▪ Draw a line under the correct pronoun.

1. Nina's father gave (her, she) a new camera.

2. She wants to learn to take pictures with (them, it).

3. (She, Her) father will show her how the camera works.

4. Nina and (she, her) dad take some pictures.

5. Nathan and (I, me) are Nina's cousins.

6. We hope she sends (we, us) copies of the photos.

Adjectives ▪ Underline each adjective.

1. Dinosaurs were once the largest reptiles on Earth.

2. Some dinosaurs ate green plants.

3. Other animals felt safer around dinosaurs that ate plants.

4. Some dinosaurs ate fresh meat.

5. It was dangerous for other animals to be close to one of these hungry dinosaurs.

Adverbs ▪ Underline each adverb.

1. Dinosaurs lived happily for a long time.

2. Scientists have carefully studied how dinosaurs lived.

3. There are no dinosaurs alive today.

4. Scientists do not know exactly what happened to them.

5. They have worked very hard to find reasons why the dinosaurs died.

Capitalizing Proper Nouns ▪ **Rewrite the words.**
Use capital letters where needed.

1. december _____

7. nova scotia _____

2. winter _____

8. vancouver _____

3. monday _____

9. thanksgiving _____

4. my sister _____

10. canada _____

5. louise _____

11. tomás _____

6. new year's day _____

12. store _____

Capitalization ▪ **Circle the letters that should be capitalized.**

1. my family lives in toronto, ontario.

2. i go to school at deer park elementary.

3. mrs. n. kelly is my teacher this year.

4. my class has been studying dinosaurs.

5. she is taking us to a museum.

6. we'll get to see dinosaur bones at the museum.

7. the museum is south of our school.

8. it is on avenue road near queen's park.

9. it is called the royal ontario museum.

10. the museum is closed on sunday and monday.

11. we're going there on the first tuesday in march.

12. mr. peterson, our principal, says we will have a great time.

Punctuation ■ **Put periods, commas, question marks, quotation marks, and apostrophes where needed.**

1. Mrs Kelly asked the people at the museum if they were ready for us

2. Yes they were ready for our class

3. We saw dinosaur bones snakes and birds at the museum

4. I didnt see all of the birds but I saw all of the dinosaurs bones

5. We watched a film about baby dinosaurs

6. Adam asked Have you ever seen a film about baby dinosaurs before

7. Hoan said No I havent

8. I liked the film the cave and the dinosaur footprints the best said Neal

9. Lets plan another trip for next month said Mrs Kelly

10. Do you think Mr Peterson will let the class come back

Parts of a Letter ■ **Rewrite the parts of a letter. Use capital letters and commas where they are needed.**

1. dear zach _____

2. june 1 1997 _____

3. moncton new brunswick e1b 4w7 _____

4. sincerely _____

5. april 9 1998 _____

6. your friend _____

7. dear jesse _____

8. moose jaw saskatchewan s6h 4c3 _____

Writing Sentences ▪ Write each thought as a sentence.

1. watching television after dinner

_____

2. laughing at the funny lines

_____

3. eating popcorn as I watch

_____

Writing Paragraphs ▪ Circle the topic sentence in each paragraph. Then number the sentences in the correct order.

_____ Next, practise saying your part in front of a

mirror. _____ The first thing you can do to make

yourself feel better is to get used to being on a stage.

_____ Finally, ask some friends or family members if

they will listen as you practise. Most people get

scared when they have to act in front of people.

_____

_____ First, some students held imaginary cameras.

_____ Yesterday Ms. Yamata's class put on a television

show. _____ After the show was over, the class

discussed what they had learned. _____ Then other

students acted out a story.

Writing a How-to Paragraph ▪ Write a paragraph that tells how to make a peanut butter and jam sandwich. Be sure to include a good topic sentence and the steps you would follow.

_____

_____

_____

_____

_____

_____

Writing a Telephone Message ▪ Read what was said in this telephone call. Then write the message Claudia might leave for Tony. Write today's date and time.

CLAUDIA: "No, I'm sorry. Tony isn't home right now. May I take a message?"

KIM: "Yes, please tell him that he needs to call me at work. The number here is 555-9487. I need to ask him about a computer problem we are having. Thank you. Goodbye."

(Date) _____

(Time) _____

(To) _____

(Message) _____

_____

(From) _____

Following Written Directions ▪ **Read the directions and study the map. Then answer the questions.**

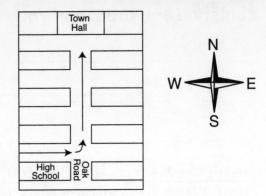

Go east past the high school.
Turn north on Oak Road.
Go three blocks until Oak Road ends.

1. Which direction do you go to pass the high school?_____

2. What is the name of the road on which you turn north?_____

3. To what building do these directions lead you? _____

Grouping ▪ **Write the words from the box under the correct heading.**

toast	spaghetti	pancakes
fish	popcorn	raisins

Breakfast   **Dinner**   **Snacks**

_____   _____   _____

_____   _____   _____

Using a Table of Contents and an Index ▪ **Answer the following questions.**

1. Where in a book would you find a table of contents?_____

2. What information does a table of contents list? _____

3. Where in a book would you find an index? _____

4. In what order are the subjects listed in an index? _____

Alphabetical Order ▪ Write each list of words in alphabetical order.

1. rake _____

   scare _____

   sat _____

2. teeth _____

   cause _____

   cheer _____

Guide Words ▪ Study the dictionary page on the right. Write the guide words for the page.

_____ / _____

leather	〰〰〰
〰〰〰	〰〰〰
〰〰〰	〰〰〰
〰〰〰	lie

Words with More Than One Meaning ▪ Read the dictionary entry for <u>batter</u>. Write the number of the meaning that is used in each sentence.

_____ 1. James mixed the <u>batter</u> for two minutes.

_____ 2. The second <u>batter</u> hit a home run.

batter 1 a mixture of flour, milk, and eggs used in cooking. **2** a player whose turn it is to bat.

Pronunciation ▪ Study each respelling using the pronunciation key. Then circle the word that matches each respelling.

1. (noi′ zē)   nose   notes   noisy

2. (dro′ ing)   growing   drawing   drowning

3. (sum′ ər)   summary   summer   simmer

4. (fus)   fuse   fuss   fish

5. (ə wer′)   beware   aware   wear

6. (on′ ər)   under   onward   honour

hat, āge, fär; let, ēqual, tėrm; it, īce; hot, ōpen, ôrder; oil, out; cup, pùt, rüle; əbove, takən, pencəl, lemən, circəs; ch, child; ng, long; sh, ship; th, thin; ᴛʜ, then; zh, measure

Index